THIRTY-ONE DAYS OF PRAYER JOURNAL *for kids*

STEFANIE BOYLES

INTRODUCTION

Prayer is an invitation to commune with God. Prayer fosters intimacy between God and His people. It is a costly gift. Because of Jesus, we have access to the throne of God. Because of His blood, we can confidently approach Him, knowing He will not turn His face from us. This means we can come before God on behalf of others. Just as Christ intercedes for us, we can intercede for others. Praying for others is a joyful responsibility and privilege, and we are blessed in the process as our hearts and minds are transformed more into His likeness. Prayer allows us to glorify God—let us be a people who pray.

This booklet is designed to guide young hearts to pray over different topics for 31 days. Each day provides a topic, prayer prompts, Scripture passage, and space to journal specific prayer requests. Each day also includes a fun activity page to accompany the daily topic and foster spiritual conversations.

DAY 1

Our Family

READ MARK 12:30-31

Our love for God leads us to love our neighbors. Our family members are our neighbors. Pray for a family member in need.

Pray for love and peace to grow in our home and that our family would show Christ to those around us.

Pray that our hope would be found in Christ alone and that this hope would give us boldness in sharing the gospel.

DRAW SOMEONE IN YOUR FAMILY WHO YOU ARE PRAYING FOR

Prayer Requests for Our Family

DAY 2

Parents

READ DEUTERONOMY 6:4-9

Pray for parents to love God with all of their heart, mind, soul, and strength.

Pray for parents to lead the home with wisdom and disciple their children as ambassadors of Christ.

Pray for parents to have strength and protection in their work inside and outside of the home.

DRAW A PORTRAIT OF YOUR FAMILY

Prayer Requests for Your Parents

DAY 3

Our Neighbors

•••••

READ I TIMOTHY 2:1–2

Pray for a neighbor who does not know Jesus as his or her Lord and Savior.

Pray for a neighbor who is hurting (physically, emotionally, etc.).

Pray that our neighborhood is a place where God's righteousness, love, and mercy are known.

COLOR THE NEIGHBORHOOD

Prayer Requests for Our Neighbors

DAY 4

Our Friends

READ ECCLESIASTES 4:12

Pray for a friend who does not know Jesus as his or her Lord and Savior.

Pray for a friend who is struggling with sin or wrestling with hurt or fear.

Pray for wisdom in how you can be a better friend in order to show others the love of Christ.

DRAW A PICTURE OF YOU AND YOUR FRIENDS

Prayer Requests for Our Friends

DAY 5

Our Leaders

READ 1 TIMOTHY 2:1-4

Pray for the pastors and elders of your church and other local churches in your city.

Pray for government leaders and those in authority.

Pray for leaders in your community: local officials, police officers, school administrators, teachers, and first responders.

DRAW SOME OF THE DIFFERENT LEADERS IN YOUR COMMUNITY

Prayer Requests for Our Leaders

DAY 6

The Local Church

READ COLOSSIANS 1:9-10

Pray for genuine love between all believers and for the gospel to unite them.

Pray for the pastors and elders to remain dedicated to God's Word and faithfully teach it.

Pray for members to grow in love and holiness in order to reflect Christ to the greater community.

DRAW A PICTURE OF WHERE YOU GO TO CHURCH

Prayer Requests for the Local Church

DAY 7

The Global Church

• • • • •

READ I PETER 2:9

Pray that God's name would be treasured throughout the entire world.

Pray that the Word of God would be the ultimate authority on truth in all churches.

Pray that all of God's people would do the will of God with zeal, humility, and purity.

COLOR THIS PICTURE OF OUR WORLD

Prayer Requests for the Global Church

DAY 8

Unreached People Groups

• • • • •

READ PSALM 96:11

There are about 230 different countries in our world, but as many as 16,000 different people groups. Pray for a country that is closed to God's Word.

Pray for a people group who has yet to hear the gospel (there are still over 7,000 unreached people groups).

Pray for God to reveal Himself in whatever way possible (missionaries, dreams, visions) to these communities.

COLOR IN JESUS' WORDS FROM MARK 16:15

GO INTO
ALL THE
WORLD AND
PREACH
THE GOSPEL
TO ALL
CREATION

Prayer Requests for Unreached People Groups

HOLY

DAY 9

Missionaries

READ ISAIAH 52:7

Pray that these missionaries will stand firm on God's Word and be filled with the Holy Spirit.

Pray that these missionaries will show Christlike character and find favor with unbelievers.

Pray for their protection and that they would persevere in the midst of hardships and suffering.

DRAW A MISSIONARY FAMILY SHARING THE GOSPEL

Prayer Requests for Missionaries

DAY 10

Gratitude

READ PSALM 136

Praise God for who He is and that we can know Him personally. God is holy, loving, gracious, merciful, and faithful.

Praise God for the gift of eternal life offered through the person and work of Jesus.

Praise God for being our provider. He is the giver of good gifts like clothes, a home, food, laughter, family, friends, and more.

DRAW YOUR FAVORITE MEAL ON THIS PLATE

Prayer Requests of Gratitude

DAY 11

Contentment

•••••

READ JOHN 16:33

Pray that the Holy Spirit will help us be satisfied in God and trust and delight in the eternal promises in His Word.

Confess anything or anyone in your heart that you love more than God. Ask Him to help you treasure Christ above all. He brings lasting peace and joy.

Pray that we will be quick to remember God's faithfulness, grace, and provision when we want to grumble or be ungrateful.

COLOR THIS PICTURE AND THANK GOD FOR HIS PROMISES

Prayer Requests for Contentment

DAY 12

People on the Fringes

READ MATTHEW 25:31-46

Choose one of the following people groups, and pray for their well-being: refugees, the homeless, the disabled, or the abused.

Ask God to help us identify ways in which we can serve those in need in our community.

Pray that these vulnerable people would feel welcomed in churches and find their needs met by the generosity of believers.

COLOR THIS PICTURE AND DISCUSS GOD'S LOVE FOR ALL PEOPLE

Prayer Requests for People on the Fringes

DAY 13

Children in Need

READ JAMES 1:27

Pray that the needs of orphans in our world today (things such as food, shelter, healthcare, and education) are met.

Pray for the children who are trapped in a bad situation. Pray for divine protection, deliverance, and healing.

Pray for the foster kids in the United States. These children have faced abuse and abandonment. Pray that God would raise up foster families to love them well and for reunification or adoption to occur.

DRAW SOMETHING THAT YOU ARE PRAYING ABOUT TODAY

Prayer Requests for Children in Need

DAY 14

Confession

READ 1 JOHN 1:9

Confess any idols in your life that are competing for the affection of your heart.

Pray that God's kindness would lead us to repentance. Take time to repent of any personal sins (lying, pride, selfishness, grumbling, etc.).

Pray that we would be quick to obey the Holy Spirit as He leads and convicts us throughout the day.

COLOR THE LITTLE GIRL PRAYING

Prayer Requests of Confession

DAY 15

Persecuted Christians

•••••

READ 1 CORINTHIANS 12:26

Pray for protection of our persecuted brothers and sisters. More than 300 Christians die every month because of their faith!

Pray for strength to endure the trials they face and that the churches in those countries would remain bold.

Pray for an extra cover of protection over Christian women who endure double persecution for their faith and gender.

COLOR AND DISCUSS THE FIRST PART OF TODAY'S VERSE

So if one member suffers, all the members suffer with it.

Prayer Requests for Persecuted Christians

DAY 16

The Great Commission

READ MATTHEW 28:16-20

Pray that the gospel would spread to every ethnic people group in the world and that all people would respond to God's kindness by putting their faith in Christ.

Pray that God would raise up missionaries to go to unreached people groups and effectively share the gospel.

Pray that our family would boldly and lovingly proclaim the gospel of Jesus through words and good deeds.

COLOR THESE PEOPLE FROM AROUND THE WORLD

Prayer Requests for the Great Commission

DAY 17

Worship

READ ROMANS 12:1-2

Pray that we would lead lives of worship and that we would love and serve God with humility.

Pray that we would treasure God above all things and enjoy Him.

Pray that our attitudes, thoughts, words, and actions would be pure expressions of worship to God.

COLOR THIS PHRASE OF PRAISE

Prayer Requests for Worship

DAY 18

Personal Growth in Godliness

READ 1 THESSALONIANS 4:3-8

Pray that our love for God will grow so much that it transforms our character and behavior to Christlikeness.

Pray that God would grow a deeper desire in us to study His Word and that we would strive to obey His Word.

Pray that our family would pursue holiness over happiness.

MAKE THIS PLANT GROW BY ADDING FLOWERS AND LEAVES

Prayer Requests for Personal Growth in Godliness

DAY 19

Our Work

•••••

READ COLOSSIANS 3:23

Pray that each of us would work with excellence in all things (schoolwork, chores, activities) even when things get hard.

Pray that each of us would use our gifts, talents, passions, and creativity in ways that bring honor and glory to God.

Pray for strength, perseverance, and diligence to do good work but also to love and respect those around us.

DRAW DIFFERENT KINDS OF WORK YOU GET TO DO

Prayer Requests for Our Work

DAY 20

Eternal Perspective

READ 1 JOHN 2:15

Pray that our family would see everything in this life as temporary and invest our lives (time, talents, desires, and more) in things that will last for eternity.

Pray that we will store up treasures in heaven and value spiritual blessings over material blessings.

Pray that we would live in such a way that it would remind others of the reality of forever and help them lift their eyes to admire God and seek Him.

COLOR THESE GLASSES AND DISCUSS ETERNAL PERSPECTIVE

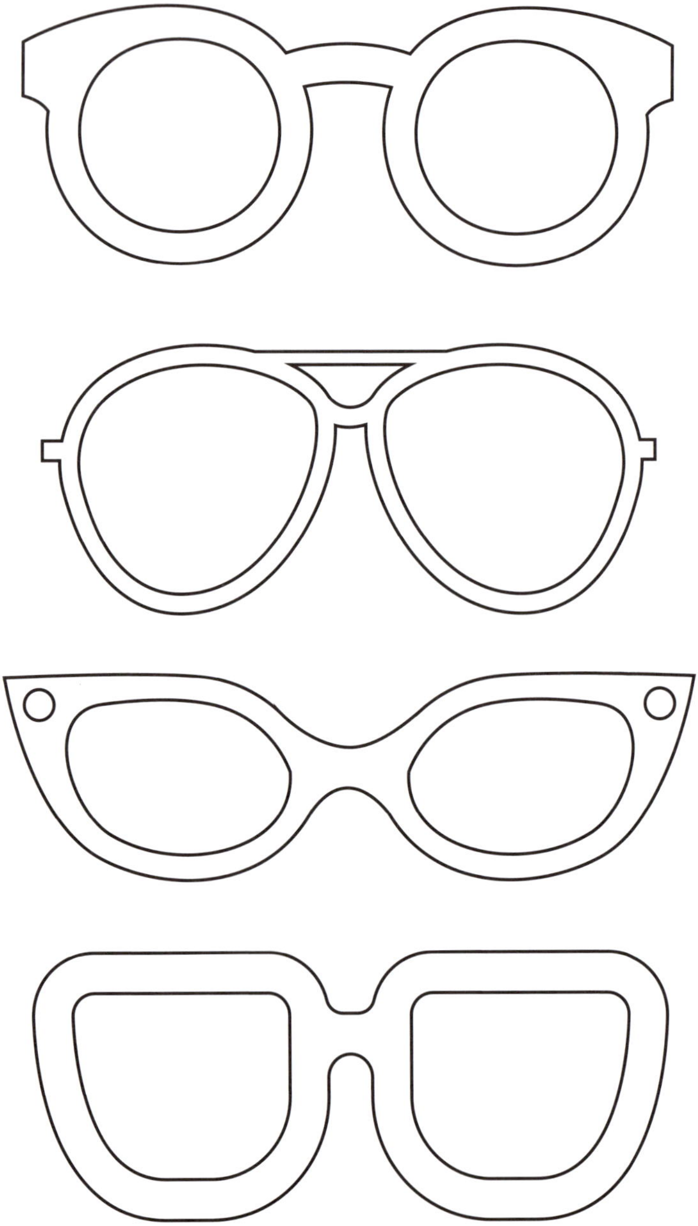

Prayer Requests for Eternal Perspective

DAY 21

Personal Character

READ GALATIANS 5:22–23

Pray that God would increase our desire to grow in Christlikeness.

Pray that God will help us turn away from sin patterns and pursue holiness with zeal.

Pray that our family models Christian character: the fruit of the Spirit, hospitality, generosity, humility, respect, forgiveness, honesty, courage, gratitude, purity, compassion, and more.

COLOR THE FRUIT AND DISCUSS THE FRUITS OF THE SPIRIT

Prayer Requests for Personal Character

DAY 22

Healing

READ PSALM 103

Pray for someone who needs physical healing.

Pray for someone who needs emotional or mental healing.

Pray for someone who needs spiritual healing.

COLOR THE HEALING HEART

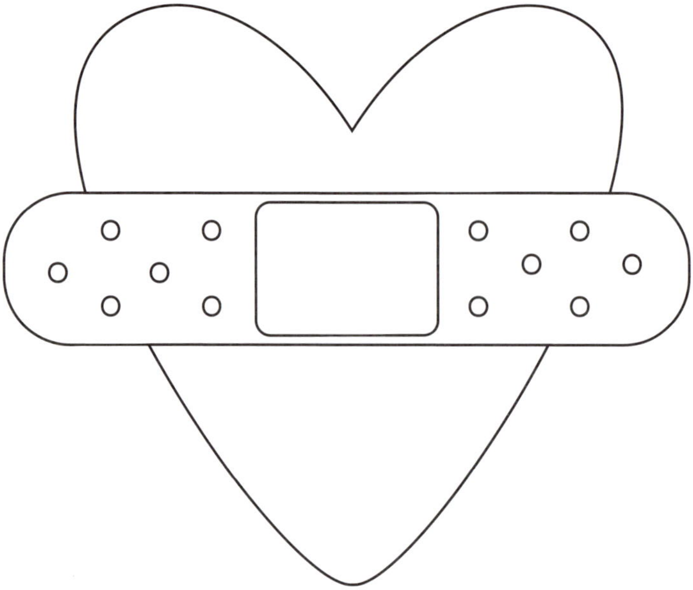

Prayer Requests for Healing

DAY 23

Personal Struggles

READ PHILIPPIANS 4:4-9

Confess any worries, fears, stress, or anxiety that you are wrestling with right now.

Pray that we would lean into Jesus and that His peace would guard our hearts and minds.

Pray that we would remember who God says we are and live out of our true identity in Jesus.

WRITE OUT PHILIPPIANS 4:7
IN THE SPACE BELOW

Prayer Requests for Personal Struggles

DAY 24

Hospitality

READ 1 PETER 4:8-9

Pray that our family would keep open hearts and an open home in order to welcome others and show them the gospel.

Pray that we would be generous with all that God has entrusted to us and that we would remember that we are only stewards.

Pray for opportunities to show others hospitality. Pray for open eyes to see where we can welcome, give, and serve.

COLOR THE FRONT PORCH AND DISCUSS WAYS TO BE HOSPITABLE

Prayer Requests for Hospitality

DAY 25

Obedience

READ JOHN 15:14

Pray that we would trust and obey God.

Pray that we would lead lives of obedience to God's Word.

Pray we would have an attitude of submission to those who God has placed over us (parents and pastors).

LIST DIFFERENT WAYS YOU CAN SHOW OBEDIENCE

Prayer Requests for Obedience

DAY 26

Patience & Trust

READ COLOSSIANS 1:11

Pray that God would bear the fruit of patience in our lives.

Pray that we would trust God and His plan so that we can wait patiently whenever needed.

Pray that we would be patient with those around us, remembering God's patience and kindness toward us.

COMPLETE THE WORD SEARCH ABOUT PATIENCE AND TRUST

MIGHT TRUST STRENGTH

JOY ENDURANCE FRUIT

PATIENCE

T	Y	W	X	G	I	A	N	N	T
Y	E	N	D	U	R	A	N	C	E
J	W	X	W	T	R	U	S	T	B
O	D	S	K	Y	Z	X	B	U	L
Y	Z	O	F	W	R	P	Y	O	S
Q	S	T	R	E	N	G	T	H	M
Q	Y	D	U	E	X	E	F	C	I
P	A	T	I	E	N	C	E	X	G
H	T	T	T	L	M	Q	B	D	H
R	W	V	J	I	T	H	P	O	T

Prayer Requests for Patience & Trust

DAY 27

Our Words & Attitudes

READ LUKE 6:45

Pray that the words that come out of our mouths would build others up and not be foul or hurtful to others.

Pray that we would have attitudes of humility and trust in God.

Pray that the love of Christ would guide our thoughts, words, and attitudes.

WRITE KIND WORDS OR GOOD ATTITUDES IN THE SPEECH BUBBLES

Prayer Requests for Our Words & Attitudes

DAY 28

Wisdom

READ JAMES 1:5

Pray and ask God for wisdom, and confess your need of Him.

Pray that God would help us understand His Word so that we can live our lives to God's glory.

Pray that we would remember God's goodness and faithfulness in the past and that we would trust Him with our future.

COLOR THE PICTURE AND DISCUSS HOW GOD'S WORD LIGHTS OUR WAY

Prayer Requests for Wisdom

DAY 29

The Lord's Prayer

READ MATTHEW 6:7-15

Pray that God would be worshiped throughout this earth and that His name would be honored and glorified.

Pray that we would yield to God's will and lead lives of joyful obedience.

Pray that we would respond to His mercy and kindness by quickly forgiving others and loving our enemies.

COLOR THE PICTURE OF JESUS TEACHING HIS DISCIPLES

Prayer Requests from the Lord's Prayer

DAY 30

Safety

READ 2 THESSALONIANS 3:3

Pray for physical, emotional, and mental protection as we go out into the world today.

Pray for spiritual protection—that our hearts would not be deceived and that the greatest desire of our hearts would be Jesus.

Pray for those protecting our cities and nation such as fire fighters, medical professionals, military, and police force.

DRAW THESE FIRST RESPONDERS AND DISCUSS HOW TO PRAY FOR THEM

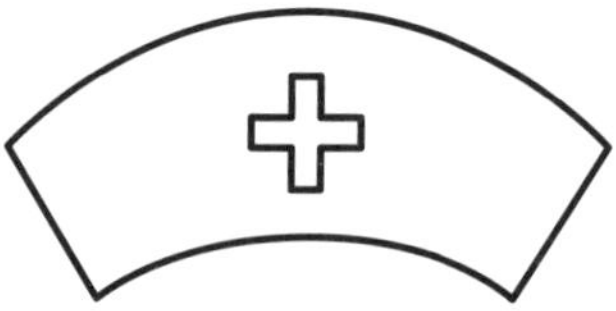

Prayer Requests for Safety

DAY 31

Preach the Gospel to Yourself

READ 2 CORINTHIANS 5:21

Confess your sins.

Praise Jesus, and thank Him for dying on the cross for the forgiveness of our sins.

Praise Jesus for who He is and what He has done and that because of that, we are declared righteous before God.

COLOR THE PICTURE AND DISCUSS TODAY'S TOPIC

Thank you for choosing this tool from The Daily Grace Co.

CONNECT WITH US

@thedailygraceco

@kristinschmucker

CONTACT US

info@thedailygraceco.com

SHARE

#thedailygraceco

#lampandlight

VISIT US ONLINE

thedailygraceco.com

MORE DAILY GRACE

the daily grace app

daily grace podcast